SOON—

AH, THIS IS WHAT I CALL SOLID COMFORT!

IT'S SOLID, ALL RIGHT!

SOMEHOW ROCK LACKS THE FRIENDLY FEEL OF SAND!

MAYBE SO, BUT IT IS PEACEFUL AND QUIET HERE! JUST THE CARESS OF THE BREEZE AND THE SOUND OF THE SURF!

IN OTHER WORDS, DULL!

THE MOST EXCITING THING WE CAN DO OUT HERE IS EAT!

THEN I SAY IT'S TIME FOR SOME EXCITEMENT! WHO WANTS HAM, AND WHO WANTS CHEESE?

AT THE RISK OF BEING CONSUMED WITH HYSTERIA, I'LL HAVE CHEESE!

FOR CRYIN' OUT LOUD! WHAT'S IT TAKE TO CHEER YOU GUYS UP, AN EXPLOSION?

WELL, NOW THAT YOU MENTION IT...

RUMBLE

WHAT THE DUM-DOODLE?

IT FEELS LIKE AN EARTHQUAKE!

IT LOOKS LIKE IT, TOO!

CRACK

TAKE IT SLOWLY, UNCA DONALD! THESE EXPOSED ROCKS ARE COVERED WITH **ALGAE**!

AS LONG AS IT DOESN'T **BITE**, I'M NOT WORRIED ABOUT IT!

BESIDES, I'M AN OLD HAND AT — WHOA! WHO **OILED** THIS ROCK?

SLIP SLIP SLIP SLIP

OOF!

SQOOSH

WE TRIED TO TELL YOU, UNCA DONALD!

THESE ROCKS ARE...

SLIP SLIP SLIP

...SLIPPERY!

OW!

HA! **NOW** WHO'S DOING THE SEA-BED TWO-STEP WITH THE PIN CUSHIO SET?

YOU!

OW!

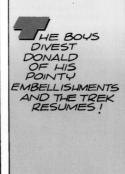

THE BOYS DIVEST DONALD OF HIS POINTY EMBELLISHMENTS AND THE TREK RESUMES!

THERE OUGHT TO BE A LAW AGAINST THOSE SABE SKINNED ASSASSINS!

KACHOOF

HEN THE CLOUD OF SAND FINALLY SETTLES—

YOU'RE OKAY, AREN'T YOU, UNCA DONALD?

ME? WHY ASIDE FROM BEING SOUSED, SOAKED, PINCHED, POKED, INKED, PECKED AND SANDED— I'M JUST *DUCKY DANDY!*

A LITTLE SARCASM, EH?

POSSIBLY A TAD!

BUT I'LL TELL YOU THIS— THE NEXT TIME ANYBODY IN THIS FAMILY GETS SOME LAME-BRAINED IDEA ABOUT HAVING A PICNIC . . .

YES?

. . . IT'S GOING TO BE HELD IN THE *KITCHEN!*

DOC STATIC'S LATEST MODERN WONDER PROVIDES MICKEY AND GOOFY WITH FOOD FOR THEIR MINDS... AND STOMACHS—

THAT'S THE *THIRD* LOAD OF APPLES I'VE *DUPLICATED* IN MY NEW *3-D COPIER!* SO FAR IT'S OPERATING PERFECTLY!

YOU SURE CAN INVENT 'EM, DOC!

YUP! THUH DUPLICATES *TASTE* LIKE THUH ORIGINALS, TOO!

ORIGINALS

COPIES

© 2000-129

WIGGLES AND GIGGLES! YOUR MACHINE EVEN COPIED A *WORM!* THAT'S GREAT— AND KINDA *GROSS!*

HEY, COULD YUH EVEN COPY... *ME?*

A *GOOFY II?!* I GUESS I CAN'T HAVE *TOO MANY* BEST PALS!

ORIGINALS

BETTER NOT TRY IT, GOOFY!

WHY NOT? I HEAR *TWO HEADS* ARE *BETTER* THAN *ONE!*

ORIGINALS

YEAH! WHY NOT? WHAT *COULD* HAPPEN?

WELL, UM—

LET'S GO FOR IT! ~OOMPH!~

ORIGINALS

~SIGH!~ I'LL START THE COPIER! I CAN'T THINK OF A *GOOD* REASON *NOT* TO TRY!

WOW! WHAT COULD BE BETTER THAN A PAL LIKE GOOFY?

TWO PALS LIKE GOOFY!

I HOPE YOU'RE RIGHT!

GAWRSH!

COPIES

I LIKE TO TELL MY FRIENDS APART, SO I'M GOING TO GIVE MY *NEW* BUDDY THIS *SCARF* TO WEAR!

I HATE TA BE THUH *PICKY* ONE, BUT I *HATE* STRIPES! THEY'RE SO... *STRIPY!*

REALLY?! I HATE STRIPES, *TOO!* HOW ABOUT A *CHEESEBURGER,* PAL?

I *LOVE* CHEESEBURGERS!

~HM!~

DO YUH LIKE *FLIP THUH FISH* COMIC BOOKS, TOO?

LOVE 'EM!

IT'S PRETTY **SPECIAL**, HAVING A TWIN! OKAY THEN, I'LL SEE YOU TWO THIS AFTERNOON!

BUT I HAFTA CONFESS I'M MIFFED AT BEING LEFT OUT OF THE NEW GOOFY CLUB!

I THOUGHT I WAS GOING TO HAVE **TWO** BEST FRIENDS NOW! INSTEAD, I HAVE **NONE**!

AND THE FISH DON'T **BITE** IN THE AFTERNOON! AND I ALREADY RESERVED THE BOAT WITH A DEPOSIT AND-AND-AND WHY DOESN'T GOOFY JUST **MARRY** GOOFY TWO?!

AFTER CALMING DOWN, MICKEY SEEKS SOME ADVICE—

IT'S **GETTING** TO ME, DOC! I DON'T WANT TO HURT MY FRIENDSHIP WITH GOOFY, BUT HE'S HAVING A **GREAT TIME** WITH **HIMSELF**!

IF IT BOTHERS YOU, MICKEY, THEN **TELL** GOOFY! HAVE A HEART-TO-HEART—I MEAN, HEART-TO-HEART-TO-HEART TALK WITH HIM—I MEAN, **THEM**!

HONESTY IS THE BEST POLICY! **I** WAS **HONEST** WHEN I THOUGHT COPYING GOOFY WAS A **BAD** IDEA IN THE FIRST PLACE!

WE **IGNORED** YOU! NOW THERE ARE **TWO** GOOFYS!

YES, BUT ⇥AHEM!⇤ **MY** CONSCIENCE IS CLEAR!

SO MICKEY DECIDES TO CLEAR HIS OWN CONSCIENCE—

HI, GOOFY...NO SCARF, SO I GUESS YOU'RE THE ORIGINAL! →HEH!←...IT MUST BE PRETTY *TERRIFIC*, HAVING A TWIN WHO LIKES ALL THE SAME THINGS *YOU* DO...

...BUT HEY, I ALWAYS THOUGHT *WE* HAD A LOT OF FUN TOGETHER, TOO! AND *NOW*— NOW I FEEL LIKE YOU AND YOUR DOUBLE ARE SO *CLOSE* THAT I...I...

→YIKES!← IT'S A GOOFY *WOODCARVING!*

→GAWRSH!← SORRY TA *SCARE* YUH, MICKEY!

YEAH! AFTER WE FINISHED THUH SELF-PORTRAIT, WE DECIDED TA MAKE A DUMMY!

BUT...WE *GET* WHUT YER TRYIN' TA SAY! MY *BEST* BUDDY IS FEELIN' *LEFT OUT!*

YER THE LAST PERSON WE'D WANNA HURT!

WE?! WHADDAYUH MEAN, *WE? YER* THE *COPY!* THIS IS ALL *YER* FAULT!

WHAT THE...?!

→HUH?!← *YER* THE ONE WHO ALWAYS WANTED A *SELF-PORTRAIT! I* LIKE *FISHIN'* WITH *MICKEY!*

ARE YOU SAYIN' *I DON'T* LIKE FISHIN' WITH MICKEY?

WELL, IF YUH *DID*, WHY DIDN'T *YOU* SUGGEST WE *GO*?

WHY DIDN'T *YOU*? AN' IF *YOU* REALLY HATE STRIPES, WHY DIDN'T YUH GET A *DIFFERENT SCARF*?

MAYBE I *KEPT* IT JUST TA *ANNOY* YUH!

WELL, IT SHURE *WORKED*!

SO *THAT'S* WHY YUH *HOGGED* THUH *TV REMOTE* ALL LAST NIGHT!

HOGGED? IT'S *MY* REMOTE! YER A *CLONE*, YUH *CLOWN*!

⇥YIKES!⇤ THEY'RE COMING TO *BLOWS*! I'D BETTER GET THEM BOTH ONTO SOME COMMON GROUND!

⇥GULP!⇤ HERE'S SOMETHING WE CAN *ALL AGREE* ON! HOW ABOUT A NICE *CHEESEBURGER*?

BUT EVEN FOOD CAN'T *QUELL* THE TWIN-GOOFY RAGE—

YUH THINK THIS IS *YOUR* BURGER? *HERE...TAKE IT!*

HOW ABOUT SOME *KETCHUP* TO GO WITH THAT *LOUSY ATTITUDE*?

OUT! *OUT*, YOU CRAZY TWINS!

COMMON GROUND! THIS IS A *BATTLEFIELD*!

WELL, *I'M* NO HAPPIER THAN I WAS BEFORE, AND *THESE* TWO ARE *MISERABLE!* WAS I *SELFISH* TO COMPLAIN?

NEXT DAY—

DOGGONE IT, I *WAS!* IT'S UP TO ME TO MAKE THEM BURY THE HATCHET...AND *NOT* IN *EACH OTHER!*

STARS AND STRIPES! IT'S A *CIVIL WAR!*

YOU GOT THUH CANDY! *I* WANT THUH *COOKIES!*

ALL *RIGHT!* WE *AGREED* TA *SPLIT* EVERYTHIN' *EVENLY!* WHUT'S *NEXT?*

IT'S MUH MOST...

...*PRIZED* POSSESSION!

MUH *COMPLETE* FLIP THE FISH *COMIC BOOK* COLLECTION WITH *ALL* THUH VARIANT COVERS!

THEY REALLY *DO* BELONG HALF TA *EACH* OF US!

BUT THEN WE'D HAVE TA *BREAK UP* THUH SET!

GOOFS, I THINK THERE'S ONLY *ONE* SOLUTION...

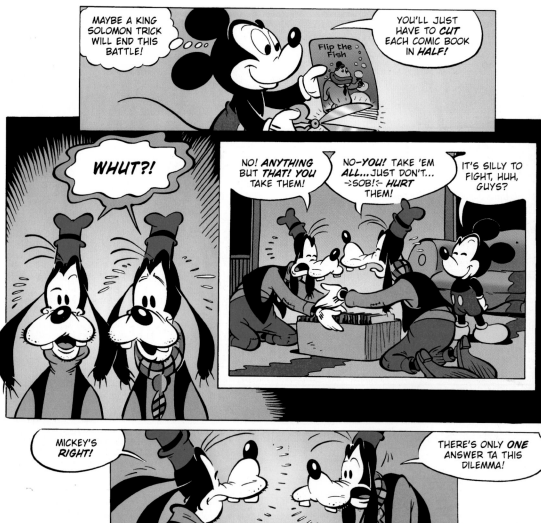

MAYBE A KING SOLOMON TRICK WILL END THIS BATTLE!

YOU'LL JUST HAVE TO *CUT* EACH COMIC BOOK IN *HALF!*

Flip the Fish

WHUT?!

NO! *ANYTHING* BUT *THAT!* YOU TAKE THEM!

NO—*YOU!* TAKE 'EM *ALL...JUST DON'T... ÷SOB!÷ HURT* THEM!

IT'S SILLY TO FIGHT, HUH, GUYS?

MICKEY'S *RIGHT!*

THERE'S ONLY *ONE* ANSWER TA THIS DILEMMA!

ONLY *ONE* GOOFY CAN STAY IN THIS TOWN!

THUH *OTHER* WILL HAVE TA *LEAVE* AN' START A *NEW LIFE!*

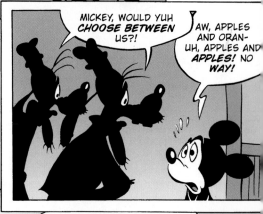

MICKEY, WOULD YUH *CHOOSE BETWEEN* US?!

AW, APPLES AND ORAN— UH, APPLES AND *APPLES!* NO *WAY!*

I WAS UPSET WHEN YOU LEFT *ME* OUT! I *CAN'T* LEAVE EITHER OF *YOU* OUT! YOU'RE *BOTH* MY BUDDY...

WAIT! COME *BACK!* I WANT YUH TA *STAY!*

YUH *MEAN* IT?

HOW COULD I STAY *MAD* AT YUH? YER SO *SMART!*

AN' *HANDSOME*

WHUT?! WE'RE *MELTIN'* TOGETHER!

~ULP!~ NOT *AGAIN!*

WHO *ELSE* LIKES GRILLED CHEESE AN' JELLY SANDWICHES?

OR KNOWS *ALL* THUH WORDS TO THUH BUNKO BEAR THEME SONG?

I, FER ONE, AM HAPPY TO BECOME *ONE* WITH SUCH A *SWELL* GUY! BUT WHUT *HAPPENED?*

~HMM!~ MUST HAVE BEEN SOME *FLAWS* IN THE DUPLICATION PROCESS! BUT I MUST SAY, I'VE NEVER BEEN *HAPPIER* AT A MISTAKE!

~HYUCK-YUK!~ IT'S GREAT TA BE ME!

SO, MICKEY! WHEN I FIX THE FLAWS, DO *YOU* WANT A TWIN? ~HA!~ A WILD *ADVENTURE-SEEKER* JUST LIKE—

~HMM!~

ER...FORGET IT, MICKEY!

The End

MORE DISNEY excitement TO COME!

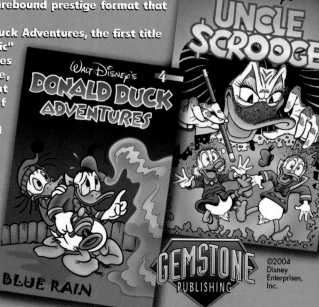

If you like this comic, you'll want to be on board for all the fun in the months to come, with Gemstone Publishing's exciting line of Disney comic books.

For collectors: Walt Disney's Comics and Stories and Uncle Scrooge, providing the best of vintage and recent classic tales by such highly-acclaimed creators as Carl Barks, Pat Block, Daniel Branca, Cesar Ferioli, David Gerstein, Michael T. Gilbert, Daan Jippes, Don Markstein, Pat McGreal, Dave Rawson, Don Rosa, Noel Van Horn, William Van Horn, and many more. These books are 64 pages and in the sturdy, squarebound prestige format that collectors love.

For readers on the go: Donald Duck Adventures, the first title in our new 5" X 7½" "Take-Along Comic" series, gives you long adventure stories starring Mickey, Donald, Scrooge, and others in modern stories that take them beyond the limits of space and time.

For readers of all ages: Donald Duck and Mickey Mouse and Friends, offering Disney fans the best contemporary Mouse and Duck stories in the familiar 32-page, stapled, comic book format.

Look for them at your local comic shop! Can't find a comic shop? Try the Toll Free Comic Shop Locator Service at (888) COMIC BOOK for the shop nearest you! If you can't find Gemstone's Disney comics in your neighborhood you may subscribe at no extra charge, and we'll pay the postage! Use the coupon below, or a copy:

©2004 Disney Enterprises, Inc.

YOU ARE A BOASTFUL PHONEY—PAH!

FFT!

POOR DONALD! IT LOOKS AS THOUGH IT WILL BE A DULL DAY, AFTER ALL

DOGGONE IT! I OVERDID THAT SHARK STORY! I WISH ANOTHER SHARK WOULD COME ALONG—NO, NO! NOT THAT!...I WISH THERE WERE SOMEBODY TO SAVE FROM DROWNING—I'D SHOW HER I'M NO PHONEY!

WE'VE GOT TO HELP UNCA DONALD! WE OWE HIM A LOT!

HE SAVED OUR LIVES

LET'S GO UP TO MINNIE MUDHEN'S—I'VE GOT AN IDEA!

HEY, MINNIE, D'YA WANTA EARN A DIME?

SURE, BUSINESS IS AWFUL!

THEN, PUT ON YOUR BATHING SUIT AND COME WITH US!

MINNIE MUDHEN'S
SYNTHETIC HAMBURGERS
PORK AND BEANS

O.K. BOYS, WHAT DO I DO NOW?

WAIT'LL WE GET CLOSE TO UNCA DONALD'S BEACH,

THEN FALL OVERBOARD...

WE WANT THAT GIRL TO SEE HIM SAVE YOU

HELP! UNCA DONALD! LADY OVERBOARD HELP!

How much is your collection worth?

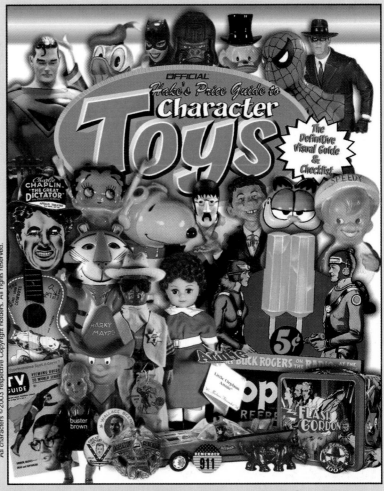

OFFICIAL
Hake's Price Guide to
Character Toys

The Definitive Visual Guide & Checklist

Find out with the Definitive Visual Guide and Checklist™!

This edition includes more than 13,000 photo illustrated entries and more than 39,000 prices in 360 unique categories! It's all in here! Toy Story, Uncle Scrooge, Spider-Man, Superman, Small Soldiers, Superhero Resins, Batman, Muhammad Ali, Disneyana, Roy Rogers, Buck Rogers, KISS, Mickey Mouse, The Lone Ranger, Puppet Master, Elvis, The Phantom, X-Men, Charlie Chaplin, The Cisco Kid, Donald Duck, Captain Marvel, Laurel & Hardy, Howdy Doody, Planet of the Apes, MAD, Hopalong Cassidy, Captain America, Toy Guns and more!

$35 (+s&h)

Available at your local comic book shop. Can't find a comic shop near you? Try the Toll Free Comic Shop Locator Service at (888) COMIC BOOK. Or you can order direct from Gemstone Publishing by calling Toll Free (888) 375-9800 ext. 249.

COMIC SHOP LOCATOR SERVICE
888-COMIC-BOOK
888-266-4226

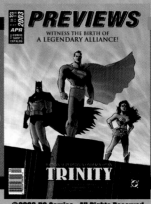

Walt Disney's Donald Duck in APPETITE FOR SUCCESS

DONALD AND HIS NEPHEWS ARE ENJOYING A RELAXING WEEKEND IN THE COUNTRY AT GRANDMA'S...

ANOTHER HELPING OF MY SECRET RECIPE STEW, DONALD?

THANKS, BUT I'M AS *STUFFED* AS UNCLE SCROOGE'S MONEY BIN! THIS IS THE *BEST MEAL* I'VE HAD SINCE, WELL...THE *LAST TIME* WE CAME TO VISIT!

000-079

NOW *THAT'S* WHAT I CALL A *GOURMET MEAL!* ->BURP!<-

LAND SAKES! IT'S JUST *DOWN-HOME, COUNTRY COOKING!*

EXACTLY! THIS IS HOW *REAL FOOD* SHOULD TASTE! NO *TRIUNSATURATED QUADRA-GLYCERIDE HEXACHLORAMINE*—JUST *FRESH INGREDIENTS FROM THE FARM!*

YOU READ THE *LABEL* ON OUR *CHOCOLATE FROSTED SUGAR BOMBS!*

I'LL HAVE YOU KNOW I AM A CONNOISSEUR OF THE CULINARY ARTS! IN FACT—SINCE I FIND MYSELF BETWEEN JOBS AT THE MOMENT—I THINK I WILL PURSUE A CAREER AS A *FAMOUS FOOD CRITIC!*

A FOOD CRITIC?! YOU!?

WHAT'S SO FUNNY ABOUT THAT!?

NOTHING! HA HA HA! IT'S JUST *LIKE* YOU TO WANT TO GET *PAID* TO *EAT!*

HMPH! THE CRITIQUING OF FOOD IS A VERY RESPECTABLE VOCATION, INFANTS! AND I INTEND TO BE THE *CREAM OF THE CROP!*

NEXT HE'LL BE AN *OPERA* CRITIC AND GET PAID TO *SLEEP!*

OR A *PERFUME* CRITIC AND GET PAID TO *BREATHE!*

UH-OH. I THINK WE JUST THREW *FAT* ON HIS *FIRE!*

NEXT MORNING...

BYE-BYE, GRANDMA! THANK YOU FOR A *FUN* AND *TASTY* WEEKEND! COME TO TOWN AND SEE US SOON!

I'LL DO THAT... SOON AS THE PLANTING'S DONE!

BACK TO MICROWAVABLE FROZEN DINNERS AND FAST FOOD. SIGH...

BUT BEFORE THAT...

The Roadkill Kafe

WE'RE *HUNGRY,* UNCA DONALD! CAN'T WE STOP FOR LUNCH?

ALL RIGHT! THAT PLACE LOOKS *BEARABLE...*

MMM-HM! SOMETHING SMELLS *GOOD,* HUH, UNCA DONALD?

THE ARCHITECTURE DOESN'T IMPRESS ME...

IT'S A *DINER!*

DÉCOR IS A BIT OUTDATED. BUT THE ATMOSPHERE IS COZY.

WHAT ARE YOU SCRIBBLING THERE, UNCA DONALD?

MY *FIRST FOOD REVIEW!* I'LL SUBMIT IT TO THE DUCKBURG TIMES WHEN WE GET HOME.

"ALTHOUGH PUNGENT AND AROMATIC, THE COMESTIBLES AT THE ROADKILL KAFE LACK A CERTAIN *JE NE SAIS QUOI*. THE VEGETABLES ARE A TRIFLE OVER-DONE AND THE SAUCES A TAD LEADEN. HOWEVER, THE PIE SELECTION'S CONTRASTING FLAVORS, COLORS, AND TEXTURES BLEND INTO A FLAVORFUL MIASMA!"

I DON'T GET IT, BUT IT *SOUNDS* GOOD!

MAYBE *THIS* CAREER WON'T END AS BADLY AS YOUR *SLOTH FARMING SCHEME!*

THE EDITOR-IN-CHIEF OF THE DUCKBURG DAILY IS EVEN MORE OPTIMISTIC...

THE DUCKBURG DAILY

HMM... PRETENTIOUSLY PERSPICACIOUS, MR. DUCK!

I'VE DINED AT THE "ROADKILL KAFE" MYSELF, AND THIS CAPTURES MY EXPERIENCE EXQUISITELY!

THANK YOU, MR. McBINGE!

I'D LIKE TO EMPLOY YOU TO SCRIVEN A REGULAR FOOD COLUMN IN MY PAPER! ARE YOU GAME?

I'M *CHAMPING* AND *MUNCHING* AT THE BIT!

HERE'S YOUR *OFFICIAL FOOD CRITIC I.D.!* IT GIVES YOU THE RIGHT TO *ADD* OR *REMOVE* STARS AT *ANY DINING ESTABLISHMENT!* BUT NOT THE SILVERWARE— HA, HA!

I WON'T DISAPPOINT! I'M A VERITABLE EINSTEIN OF EATING!

I'M ON THE ROAD TO *FAME* AND *FREE EATS!* AFTER THIS, MAYBE I'LL BECOME A *TV* CRITIC AND GET PAID TO *WATCH TV!*

DAISY!

HI, DONALD!

GUESS WHAT? I'M THE NEWSPAPER'S NEW FOOD CRITIC! DUCKBURG'S *EPICURE OF ESCARGOT! ANALYZER OF ANTI-PASTO! REVIEWER OF RAVIOLI! GOURMAND OF GOULASH!*

I'M SO HAPPY FOR YOU, DONALD!

SO WHAT ARE *YOU* UP TO IN THOSE CUTE OVERALLS WITH ALL THAT PAINT?

FUNNILY ENOUGH, *I'M* IN THE FOOD BUSINESS *TOO*, NOW!

I'M OPENING MY OWN LITTLE JUICE BAR! HOW D'YOU LIKE MY NEW SIGN?

WOW! LOVE THE AWNING!

Daisy's Juice Shack

WHY DON'T *YOU* BE MY *FIRST GUEST?* SIT DOWN AND MAKE YOURSELF AT HOME! I'LL SERVE YOU THE *HOUSE SPECIAL!*

WELL, WELL, IF TODAY ISN'T MY *LUCKY DAY!*

NOW DON'T BE *SHY*. GIVE ME YOUR *HONEST* OPINION! I MADE EVERYTHING *ALL BY MYSELF!*

DROOL...

⌐GLMPH!⌐

"GLMPH"!? AND WHAT EXACTLY DOES *THAT* MEAN, DONALD!?

WELL...UM... ⌐CHOKE!⌐ ⌐GURGLE!⌐ IT MEANS, UM... ⌐COUGH, COUGH!⌐

IS SOMETHING *WRONG?* DIDN'T I PUT ENOUGH *JALAPEÑOS* IN THE *ARCHIPELAGO DRESSING?*

I DON'T UNDERSTAND IT! *YOU* LOVED THE FOOD, DIDN'T YOU?

ER...IT WAS *ABSOLUTELY UNFORGETTABLE!* →COUGH, CHOKE!←

GOOD. THEN YOU'LL GIVE "DAISY'S JUICE SHACK" A *FULL REVIEW* IN YOUR FAMOUS COLUMN, WON'T YOU? *THAT* OUGHTTA DRUM UP SOME BUSINESS!

ER... SURE, DAISY!

WOMAN TROUBLE AGAIN, YOUR CONNOISSEUR-SHIP?

I'M DOOMED! IF I WRITE THE *TRUTH,* NOBODY WILL *EVER* EAT AT "DAISY'S JUICE SHACK" BUT IF I *LIE,* EVERYBODY WILL GO THERE...

...AND *AS SOON AS THEY TASTE HER FOOD,* MY CAREER WILL BE IN *ASHES!*

TRUE! HE'S BURNED IF HE DO, BURNED IF HE DON'T!

UNLESS...

THE DAY OF THE REVIEW DAWNS...

TO THINK I THOUGHT *FLIES IN THE SOUP* WERE THE *WORST HAZARDS* OF THIS JOB!

WAK?!

THERE HE IS! GET READY FOR LIVE BROADCAST!

W-WHAT'S GOING N, DAISY? YOU DIDN'T AY ANYTHING ABOUT *TV COVERAGE!*

WELL, I JUST *HAPPENED* TO MENTION YOU WERE COMING AND THEY *JUMPED* AT THE CHANCE TO FILM A *MASTER FOOD CRITIC* AT WORK!

JUST DON'T FLATTER ME *TOO* MUCH, DONALD! THAT WOULD BE EMBARRASSING!

⇥GULP! SWALLOW!⇤

READY WHEN YOU ARE, MR. DUCK!

ER... WELL, HERE I AM AT DAISY'S CHARMING LITTLE "JUICE SHACK"! IT'S SO *HOMEY* HERE, *EATING* THE FOOD SEEMS *SUPERFLUOUS!* ⇥COUGH!⇤

⇥GULP!⇤ BUT MY FIRST DISH IS, UM...A CHICKEN SANDWICH...ER...SERVED ON A *VERY NICE PLATE!*

I WILL BE EATING THIS CHICKEN SANDWICH, MOMENTARILY... ⇥GULP!⇤... *ISN'T IT TIME FOR A COMMERCIAL YET!?*

WHY'S HE STALLING? TAKE A BITE, ALREADY!

???

AND...AND THIS SANDWICH IS ELICIOUS! *SCRUMPTIOUS!* RICH, DOWN-HOME COUNTRY COOKING! THE BEST I'VE HAD SINCE... SINCE...

...AND THIS *SUPERB* BLACKBERRY COBBLER ROUNDS OFF A *PERFECT* DINING EXPERIENCE HERE AT "DAISY'S JUICE SHACK"!

CUT! SAM, GET READY TO INTERVIEW THE PROPRIETOR!

The End

Walt Disney's Daisy Duck in ONE FOR THE BOOKS

DAISY HAD BEEN LOOKING FORWARD TO HER FIRST DAY AS A TEMPORARY ASSISTANT AT DUCKBURG PUBLIC LIBRARY, BUT...

BOY, IS THIS *DULL!*

IS IT *ALWAYS* THIS QUIET, MISS LOGAN?

SHHHHH!

RETURNED BOOKS

07252

EVEN THE OLD MAN OVER THERE HAS FALLEN ASLEEP! MIND YOU, HE'S BEEN HERE FOR HOURS AND...

SHHHHH! JUST PUT THESE BOOKS BACK ON THE SHELVES!

I'LL BE OFF TO LUNCH NOW! YOU JUST CARRY ON MOVING THOSE RETURNS! THINK YOU CAN COPE ON YOUR OWN?

ER, I THINK SO!

RETURNED BOOKS

UT YOU WON'T BE LONG, WILL YOU?

SHHHHH!

MOMENTS LATER...

OH! CAN I HELP YOU?

I'M, *ER,* LOOKING FOR A BOOK... *"TREASURES OF THE NILE!"*

I CAN TAKE YOU RIGHT TO IT! THAT'S ONE OF THE BOOKS THAT WAS RETURNED THIS MORNING! I'VE ONLY JUST PUT IT BACK ON THE SHELF!

GREAT! LET ME HAVE IT!

HERE IT IS!

I'LL TAKE IT!

ADVENTURE

HEY! I HAVE TO STAMP THAT BOOK BEFORE I CAN LET YOU TAKE IT OUT!

FORGET IT, LADY! I'M GONE!

MUST BE A GREAT BOOK IF YOU'RE SO EAGER TO READ IT! BUT I MUST SEE YOUR LIBRARY CARD BEFORE YOU TAKE ANY BOOK OFF THE PREMISES!

NO CHANCE

I'LL CUT HIM OFF AT THE BIOGRAPHY SECTION!

I'M SORRY, BUT NOBODY LEAVES THIS LIBRARY WITH AN UNSTAMPED BOOK!

PERSISTENT, AIN'T YA?!

SO I FORGOT MY CARD! IS THAT SUCH A BIG DEAL? I'LL BRING IT IN LATER!

NO CARD, NO BOOK! LIBRARY POLICY!

SO I'LL TAKE THAT!

HEY! KEEP YOUR MITTS OFF!

NOW HAND OVER THOSE DIAMONDS OR YOU'LL BE SORRY!

N-NO WAY! THEY'RE LIBRARY PROPERTY UNTIL THE *PROVEN OWNER* SHOWS UP...

...SO *YOU'RE* NOT GETTING THEM!

YOU'RE MAKIN' ME MAD, MISSY

IF I CAN JUST SLOW HIM DOWN...

YEOOOOW!

YES!

CRASH!

YOU'RE GONNA REGRET THAT!

AND YOU'RE GONNA REGRET *THIS!*

THAT'LL BUY ME SOME TIME!

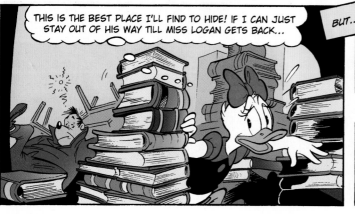

THIS IS THE BEST PLACE I'LL FIND TO HIDE! IF I CAN JUST STAY OUT OF HIS WAY TILL MISS LOGAN GETS BACK...

BUT...

OH N

NOW THERE'S A BOOK THAT REALLY **WORKS**!

A QUICK CALL TO THE POLICE, AND...

WELL, THAT JUST ABOUT WRAPS UP THE CASE! THANKS FOR YOUR HELP, MISS!

DON'T FORGET THIS! AS A PIECE OF EVIDENCE, IT'S QUITE A TREASURE!

I'LL BE OFF! I EXPECT YOU'LL BE GLAD TO GET THE LIBRARY BACK TO NORMAL AFTER THIS!

WELL, MY BOSS WILL BE BACK SOON, AND SHE'S **SO** PARTICULAR!

WELL, THAT WASN'T SUCH A DULL DAY AFTER ALL!

SOON...

OH, MISS LOGAN! THANK GOODNESS YOU'RE BACK!

SHHHHH!

YOU'LL NEVER BELIEVE WHAT JUST HAPPENED...

WHATEVER IT WAS, IT SHOULDN'T HAVE PREVENTED YOU FROM RETURNING THOSE BOOKS TO THE SHELVES! NOW **SHHHHH**!

WHAT ON EARTH...

MISS LOGAN, YOU WOULDN'T BELIEVE ME IF I TOLD YOU!

THE JR WOODCHUCKS

in

HOW MUCH WOOD WOULD A WOODCHUCK CHUCK?

...AS, THERE ARE NO MORE INTERESTING MERIT BADGES LEFT TO CHALLENGE DUCKBURG'S WOODCHUCK TROOPS! THEY'VE EARNED THEM ALL...

THE *SKYDIVING/SOUFFLÉ-MAKING* MERIT BADGE? DONE!

THE *TALL-TALE-TELLING* PRE-POLITICO-PREENING BADGE? DONE!

THE *EMERGENCY-OPEN-HEART-FIELD-SURGERY-WITH-TWEEZERS* BADGE? DONE!

99071

WE'RE *BORED,* MEN! WE'RE *AWASH* IN ENNUI!

WELL, WE *ARE* WOODCHUCKS! WHY NOT ANSWER THE AGE-OLD QUESTION AND SEE HOW MUCH *WOOD* WE CAN *CHUCK?*

YOU MEAN, HAVE A *WOOD-STACKING* CONTEST?

YEAH! A *CONTEST!*

WE'LL SPLIT INTO *TEAMS* AND SELL *TICKETS* TO *SUPPORTERS* AND RAISE MONEY FOR A NEW *MESS HALL!*

THAT'S A *GREAT* IDEA!

SO ARE BORN PLANS FOR A FINE EVENT...

AS SOON AS OUR FOUR TEAMS HAVE ENOUGH *SPONSORSHIP* AND *SUPPORT*, WE'LL SET A SANCTIONED DATE WITH THE WOODCHUCK UPPER ECHELON!

SOON...

SURE, BOYS! I'LL BE *HAPPY* TO CONTRIBUTE A PLEDGE! LET ME KNOW WHEN THE CONTEST *IS*, AND I'LL BE THERE WITH BELLS ON TO CHEER FOR YOU!

WELL, *CERTAINLY!* I'D BE *GLAD* TO CONTRIBUTE TO A FINE CAUSE LIKE THAT! I WOULDN'T MISS IT FOR THE *WORLD!*

EASY COME, EASY GO! WILL *THIS* BE ENOUGH?

SNAG

I TOLD YA WE COULD COUNT ON GLADSTONE!

SURE! BOLIVAR AND I WILL PERSONALLY ROOT YOU ON, TOO!

FINALLY COMES THE BIG DAY! SUPPORTERS FILL THE STANDS, JUDGES MOUNT THE PODIUM...

THERE'S EVEN AN *OBSERVER* FOR THE *CHICKADEE PATROL!*

OT DOGS & LEMONADE

LADIES AND GENTLEMEN, I AM THE RIGHT-HONORABLE JUNIOR WOODCHUCK *I. M. P.*! I WILL BE PRESIDING OVER TODAY'S CONTEST...

*IMAGINED MAGNIFICENT PERSON

...WHICH I HEREBY DECLARE OFFICIALLY *UNDERWAY!*

THE WINNER OF TODAY'S CONTEST WILL BE THE TEAM WHICH HAS THE MOST WOOD *PROPERLY* STACKED AT THE END OF THE ALLOTTED TIME!

HOT DOGS & LEMONADE

LET'S *AT* IT, MEN! *HUP!*

⇥UNGH!⇤

⇥UUUFFF!⇤

⇥YOW!⇤

WONK!

SAY! THAT *SMARTS!*

THERE'S GOTTA BE A *BETTER* WAY TO GO ABOUT THIS!

I SAY WE... ⇥BUZZ! MUMBLE!⇤

WE NEED TO SET UP... ⇥WHISPER!⇤

IT DOESN'T TAKE LONG FOR WOODCHUCKS TO FIGURE OUT THE BEST WAY TO "CHUCK" THE WOOD...

NOW WE'RE COOKIN'!

HUP!

HUP!

TO PROPERLY STACK THE WOOD, THE WOODCHUCKS MUST FOLLOW THE CLASSIC METHOD THAT FORESTERS HISTORICALLY USED!

TO LAST THROUGH HARD WINTERS, THE STACK MUST BE SELF-SUPPORTING AND ALMOST IMPENETRABLE!

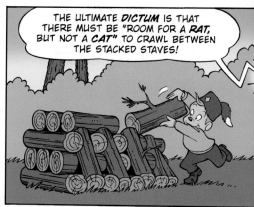

THE ULTIMATE DICTUM IS THAT THERE MUST BE "ROOM FOR A RAT, BUT NOT A CAT" TO CRAWL BETWEEN THE STACKED STAVES!

GOSH! LOOK AT THOSE FELLOWS! THEY'RE ON THEIR WAY!

BUT NOT FOR LONG!

AND SO IT GOES, UNTIL...

OKAY! THAT'S IT! TIME'S UP!

IT'S TIME TO LOOSE THE TRAINED *RAT* AND *CAT!*

THE RAT WILL RUN BETWEEN THE *GAPS* IN OUR STACKS OF WOOD...

...AND SUCCESS WILL BE OURS IF THE *CAT* IS *UNABLE* TO FOLLOW!

AT NO TIME IS THERE ANY *DANGER* TO THE RAT! THIS IS A TIME-HONORED *TRADITION* TO REMIND US OF OUR *ANCESTORS* AND THEIR ANCIENT CONCERNS—

HIYA, TOOTS! SORRY I'M LATE!

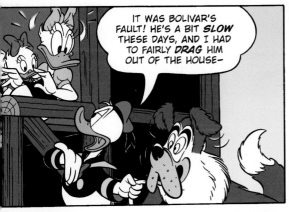

IT WAS BOLIVAR'S FAULT! HE'S A BIT *SLOW* THESE DAYS, AND I HAD TO FAIRLY *DRAG* HIM OUT OF THE HOUSE—

-:GRRRRRRR!:-

-:WAK!:-

BOLIVAR! COME *BACK* HERE!

HE'S GOING AFTER THE CAT! HE'LL RUIN *EVERYTHING!*

WE WANT OUR **PLEDGE MONEY** BACK!

WE ALREADY **SPENT** IT ON A NEW **MESS HALL!** AND BESIDES, WHY BE **MAD** AT US?!

WE ONLY **WANTED** TO GET RID OF OUR **BOREDOM!** OUR SAFE, HARMLESS CONTEST **FLOPPED,** BUT IT'S NOT LIKE ANYONE **SUFFERED** FROM—

I GUESS OUR BRILLIANT CONTEST WASN'T SO **SAFE,** AFTER ALL!

...AND GO...

I'LL DRIVE THIS BUSHEL TO THE SOUP KITCHEN AND COLLECT YOUR MONEY, BOYS!

SWELL! ⇥SIGH!⇤ AT THIS RATE, WE'LL PEEL ENOUGH SPUDS TO REPAY OUR SPONSORS **SOMETIME** NEXT CENTURY!

DON'T BE GLUM! SCROOGE, GUS, DAISY AND I AREN'T MAD AT YOU! YOU NEEDN'T REPAY **US!**

⇥SIGH!⇤ I'M **BORED!**

AW, **SHUT UP!**

UNTIL TODAY, **WE** HAD WAYS TO BE BORED THAT **DIDN'T** INVOLVE **WORK!**

AND IF WE'RE LUCKY THOSE DAYS WILL **RETURN** BEFORE WE'RE TOO **OLD AND GRAY** TO ENJOY THEM!

FLIPPABLE!
FACTUAL!
FUNCTIONAL!

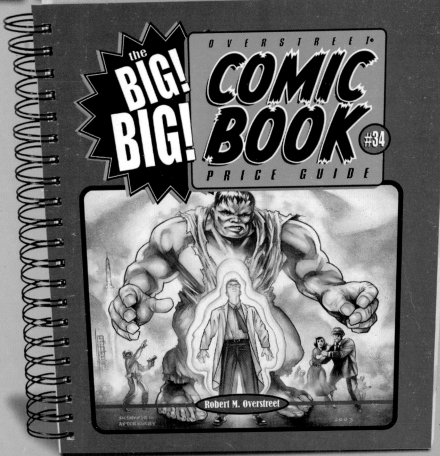

It's **The Official Overstreet Comic Book Price Guide #34** in a special limited edition! Featuring a stunning re-creation of Jack Kirby's cover for *Incredible Hulk #1* by John K. Snyder III (*Green Lantern: Brightest Day/Darkest Night*), this edition contains only the pricing, Top Ten charts, selected glossary and text from the regular edition of the *Guide*.

SPECIAL FEATURES

Stay-Flat Spiral Binding ▼ Larger Print ▼ Room For Notes ▼ A Must For Serious Collectors

SC $37